O U R
C H A N G I N G
W O R L D

The ROCK POOL

by DAVID BELLAMY

with illustrations by Jill Dow

Clarkson N. Potter, Inc./Publishers

DISTRIBUTED BY CROWN PUBLISHERS, INC., NEW YORK

It's a fine day by the sea and there's a lot to do. When you get tired of building sandcastles and playing, you can always go exploring.

The girl has seen a stranded jellyfish drying out in the seaweed and shells near today's high tide mark. She is going to get her pail to carry the jellyfish to the rock pool.

She's very careful not to touch the jellyfish with her bare hands because it might sting her.

At high tide, most of the beach is covered with water. The sea washes in and out of the rock pool twice a day. There are hundreds of living things in the pool waiting to be discovered. All you have to do is look.

The water in the pool is so clear you can see right down to the bottom. Look carefully – a large starfish and a small fish called a blenny are hiding in the seaweed. Even the shells can hold surprises. The whelk shell is used by a hermit crab as a home to protect the rear of its body, which has no hard covering. When the crab is disturbed it retreats inside the shell and closes up the entrance with its large claw.

1 starfish
2 blenny
3 whelk shell

The jellyfish is now floating among the seaweeds in the pool. Its tentacles are covered with thousands of stinging cells. These are used to paralyze small creatures before it eats them. The blenny had better stay out of the way! Crabs and starfish are protected from stings by their tough outer coverings.

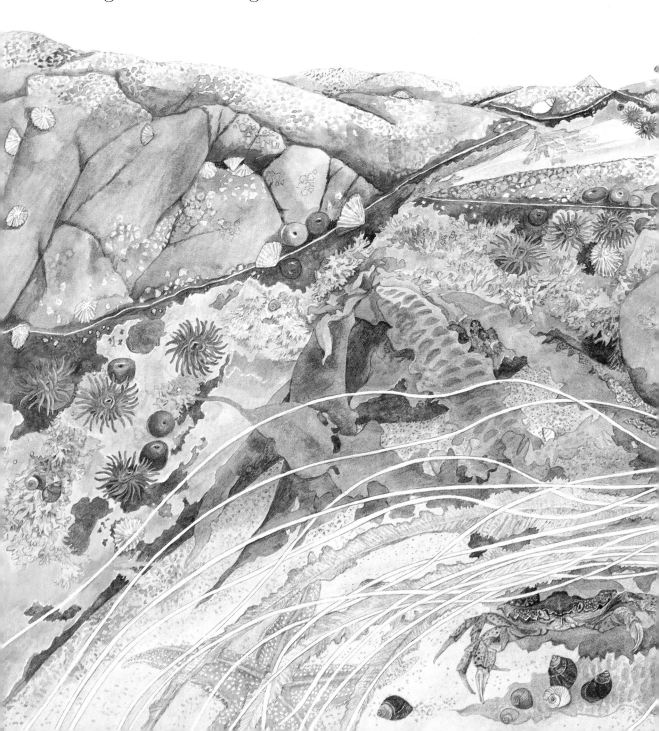

The red sea anemones are relatives of the jellyfish. They unfurl their frills of stinging tentacles in the water in search of very tiny fish and shellfish to eat.

The rocks are covered with seaweeds of all shapes and sizes. They cling to the rocks with pads called holdfasts that firmly anchor the plants. Their slippery fronds slide about in the waves without getting torn. The brown kelps and wracks are tough and can live out of water for short periods. The red seaweeds are more delicate and live only in the deepest parts of the pool.

While the tide is out, the whelks and periwinkles stay either in the pool or in the dampness under the seaweeds on the rocks. During the day, seaweeds make oxygen, which the animals in the pool need in order to live. The green seaweeds produce lots of silvery bubbles that contain oxygen.

The limpets on top of the rocks have clamped themselves down so that they won't dry up when the tide is out, but the ones in the water are moving around slowly. Can you see their feelers? Limpets graze on small seaweeds near their home base; they leave a trail of tiny marks. All the limpets will clamp down tightly in stormy weather, or if threatened by a gull.

Limpets, whelks, and periwinkles are members of the snail family. So are mussels and oysters, although they have two

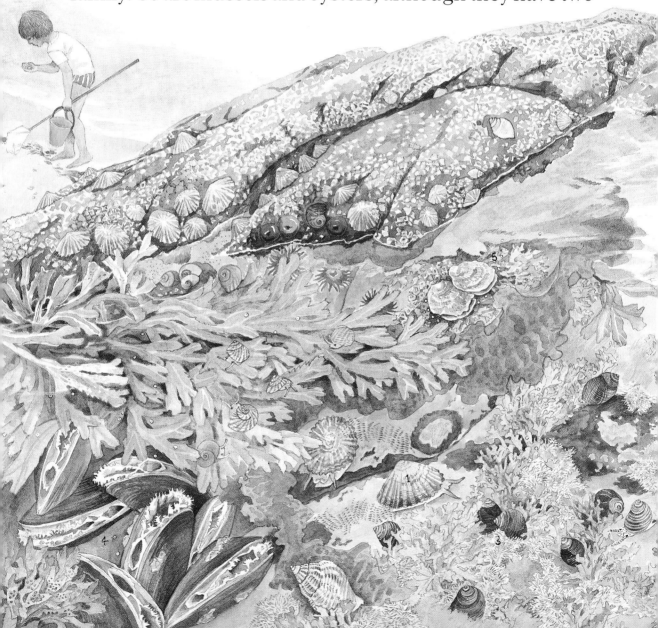

shells instead of only one. Mussels and
oysters feed by opening their hinged shells
and drawing water through, filtering out
tiny particles of food. This action also helps
keep the water in the pool clean. The
mussels can't move away because
they are anchored to the rock
by strong threads.

1 limpet 2 whelk
3 periwinkle 4 mussel
5 oyster

As crabs grow, they have to get rid of their old shells and grow new ones, one size larger. The crab hiding in a crevice is waiting for its new shell to harden before it will come out to feed. You can see its old shell on the bottom of the pool.

1 crab   2 barnacle
3 shrimp

Shrimps and prawns have lighter shells than crabs, and they can dart about quickly to catch their food.

The barnacles you can see on the rocks, and even on top of some of the limpets, may look like snails but they are related to shrimps and crabs. Look closely and you'll see their tiny feathery legs sticking out of the opening at the top; these scoop food particles from the water. If you could put your ear very close to the pool you'd be able to hear the rustle of those tiny legs.

The starfish are feeding. One is using its long tube feet to ease open the shells of mussels so that it can eat the soft parts inside. The spiky creatures on the rocks are sea urchins, relatives of the starfish. They have tube feet, too, and they move around the pool scraping up anything that is good to eat. If you go paddling, watch out for sea urchins – they can't eat you, but their spines are sharp.

This hermit crab has outgrown its old shell and is in the middle of moving house. It had better be quick – a big crab is waiting to pounce.

1 starfish
2 sea urchins
3 hermit crab

Many small fish are trapped in the pool when the tide goes out. Some are hiding among the weeds, but flat fish like plaice and flounders lie on the bottom, partly buried in the sand. They can change the pattern and color of their skin, blending with the habitat so they can lie hidden from their prey and from their enemies.

The female stickleback has laid her eggs in a nest made of seaweed, and the male is wafting clean water, full of oxygen, through the nest with his fins.

1 gunnel fish   2 plaice   3 stickleback   4 blenny

It's late afternoon and a storm is brewing. The sailboats are hurrying back to the shelter of the bay, and the people on the beach have all gone home.

The tide is coming in now and big waves are crashing on the rocks by the pool. The mussels will need their strong anchor threads and the limpets will have to clamp down and hold on very tightly until the storm is past.

There'll be no fun on the beach today.
During last night's storm, oil leaked from a struggling
tanker and washed up on the beach. Now everything
is covered with the thick black oil.

Oil is bad enough on your clothes and skin, but for the animals of the seashore it is a disaster. It clogs the gills of sticklebacks, shrimps, and crabs so they can't breathe. It sticks the seabirds' feathers together so they can't fly and, if the birds preen themselves, they will swallow oil and die. The lucky ones are washed up on the shore and taken away to be cleaned, but, for many, help has come too late.

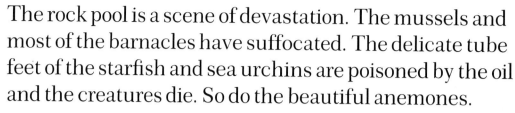

The rock pool is a scene of devastation. The mussels and most of the barnacles have suffocated. The delicate tube feet of the starfish and sea urchins are poisoned by the oil and the creatures die. So do the beautiful anemones.

Only a few creatures escape. Let's hope the fish swam out to sea before it was too late. The hermit crab is out of danger and some of the limpets have

survived, tightly clamped down until the worst of the pollution had passed. They are now grazing on the seaweed in safe places between the oil slicks.

Each high tide will wash away some of the oil, but the surviving inhabitants of the rock pool will have to live a life tainted with oil for a long time to come.

A year later, the rock pool is getting back to normal. There are more green seaweeds than before because they grow very quickly and there are fewer limpets to eat them. Thousands of tiny barnacles cover the rocks and there are new colonies of mussels in the crevices. Blennies are back again too.

The return of life to the pool may seem miraculous, but it is the way of nature to cleanse, heal, and recolonize. Let us hope that the creatures that live here will never have to face such a disaster again.